A Marvelous Guide to the Wizarding World of Harry Potter

2022 Edition ©

Edited by: Rachelle Murphy and Jodie Graham
Written by: Chelsea Hart, Jenna Konkel, Molly Davis, Quinn Lacy, Sonya D'Aulerio, Brenda Schruefer, Brittany Lapicki, Maria Beehner

Presented by Marvelous Mouse Travels
A Diamond Agency for Universal Parks and Resorts

TABLE OF CONTENTS

COPYRIGHT NOTICE	2
INTRODUCTION	3
MEET THE AUTHORS	5
PREPARE FOR YOUR TRIP	10
WIZARDING WORLD OF HARRY POTTER	13
HOGSMEADE	14
DIAGON ALLEY	25
WAND GUIDE	35
SECRETS	38
BUTTERBEER	47
THE WIZARDING WORLD OF HARRY POTTER, 1-DAY 2-PARK ITINERARY	53
WIZARDING WORLD CHALLENGE	57
FAQ'S	58
BEST WIZARDING WORLD PHOTO SPOTS	62
CONCLUSION	63
THE MARVELOUS DIFFERENCE	64
MORE FUN	65
ADDITIONAL RESOURCES	67

COPYRIGHT NOTICE

Copyright © 2021-2022 Marvelous Mouse Travels. All Rights Reserved. Any part of this book may not be reproduced or transmitted electronically without the express written permission of Marvelous Mouse Travels, unless for personal use. This guide is not endorsed by nor a product of Universal Orlando Resort. The illustrations and photographs in this guide are original or have been properly licensed.

DISCLAIMER

This book is intended for educational and entertainment purposes and is based on the authors' expertise, research, personal experiences, and opinions. Every effort has been undertaken to ensure the accuracy of the information presented in this book at the time of print. Marvelous Mouse Travels and the authors do not make any representation or warranties of any kind and do not assume any liability where it concerns the accuracy or completeness of the contents of this book. The authors will not, under any circumstances, be held liable to any person or entity with respect to any loss or incidental or consequential damages caused, or alleged to have been caused, directly or indirectly, by the information contained herein.

The content of this book is subject to change, and therefore, the publisher and authors do not accept any responsibility for any omissions or errors should they be present.

CONTACT US

If you have questions about this book or a Universal Orlando Resort vacation, please reach out to info@marvelousmousetravels.com.

INTRODUCTION

Hello Muggles, Wizards and Witches! We are so excited that you have found this guide to help you with making the most of your time in the Wizarding World at Universal Orlando Resort!

On June 18, 2010, Universal Orlando Resort officially opened The Wizarding World of Harry Potter. If you are a Harry Potter fan, you will feel like you are part of the movies inside Diagon Alley and Hogsmeade. If you are not a Harry Potter fan, you are sure to be one after your visit! There is so much to experience, and we don't want you to miss a thing!

In this guide you will learn everything you need to know about the Wizarding World including:

- How to Prepare
- Best Photo Locations
- Butterbeer Guide
- Itineraries
- Easter Eggs
- Wand Guide
- Ride Intensity Meter
- Where to Eat
- What to Buy
- And **MORE!**

How do we know so much about this amazing area?

The writers of this guide are all travel agents with Marvelous Mouse Travels. But don't let the 'mouse' in our name fool you. Marvelous Mouse Travels was named the 2019 Top Travel Agency for Universal! Although there was not a ceremony in

2020 due to the pandemic, in 2021, Marvelous Mouse Travels become the first and only Diamond Travel Agency with Universal; this means we have received the highest designation as a result of our sales and knowledge!

Not only are the Marvelous Mouse Travels' agents knowledgeable, but many have annual passes and vacation to the parks in addition to the many trainings that are attended each year! Many of them also designate themselves as "potterheads" and proudly display their "House" on shirts, hats, lanyards and robes!

Did you know that when you book with a Marvelous Mouse Travels' agent, their services are included at NO COST?

Universal Orlando builds the price of using a travel agent into every package, whether you use one or not. Some muggles make the mistake of booking online and missing out on those special extras that every Wizard and Witch needs to make their trip EPIC!

Here are just a few additional reasons to book with a Marvelous Mouse Travels' agent:

- Free Personal Concierge
- Tips and Strategies Provided
- Firsthand Experience Knowledge
- Get Early Park Admission to the Wizarding World
- Discount Monitoring
- Support a Small Business

For more information or a no-obligation vacation quote, contact Marvelous Mouse Travels at info@marvelousmousetravels.com or one of the agents directly through their email listed next to their names below.

MEET THE AUTHORS

Kari Dillon

(info@marvelousmousetravels.com)

Favorite Ride: Hagrid's Magical Creatures Motorbike Adventure

Kari is the owner of Marvelous Mouse Travels. Her love for Universal has allowed her to develop an excellent partnership with Universal. As a Diamond Agency with Universal, we are equipped to assist you in planning the perfect vacation!

Rachelle Murphy

(rachelle@marvelousmousetravels.com)

Fairhope, Alabama

Favorite Ride: Hagrid's Magical Creatures Motorbike Adventure

Rachelle is a Co-Editor of this guide and has been an agent since May 2016. Her favorite thing about the Wizarding World of Harry Potter is the Death Eaters that roam Hogsmeade and the Dark Arts at Hogwarts castle show in October!

Jodie Graham (jodie.graham@marvelousmousetravels.com)

Davidson, North Carolina

Favorite WWOHP Drink: Fire Whisky with Strongbow

Jodie is a Co-Editor of this guide and has been an agent since May 2017. Her favorite thing about the Wizarding World of Harry Potter is the incredible theming and all of the secret details to be found throughout.

Jenna Konkel
(jenna@marvelousmousetravels.com)
Clermont, Florida

Favorite Type of Butterbeer: Hot

Jenna has been an agent since July 2018. Her favorite thing about the Wizarding World of Harry Potter is watching people enter Diagon Alley for the first time! Did you know most people walk right past the entrance during their first visit?! Will you?

Maria Beehner (maria@marvelousmousetravels.com)

Long Island, New York

Favorite WWOHP Drink: Dragon Scale

Maria has been an agent since December 2015. Her favorite thing about the Wizarding World of Harry Potter are all of the stores in Diagon Alley, especially Ollivander's Wand Shop and Florean Fortescue's Ice-Cream Parlour. YUMMY!!!!

Sonya D'Aulerio (sonya@marvelousmousetravels.com)

Horsham, Pennsylvania

Favorite Type of Butterbeer: Frozen

Sonya has been an agent since November 2016. Her favorite thing about the Wizarding World of Harry Potter is that it makes her feel like a kid again!

Molly Davis

(molly@marvelousmousetravels.com)

Orlando, Florida

Favorite Ride: Hagrid's Magical Creatures Motorbike Adventure

Molly has been an agent since 2017. Her favorite thing about the Wizarding World of Harry Potter is how immersed you feel when you step inside both Diagon Alley and Hogsmeade. It is truly a very special place to visit!

Chelsea Hart

(chelsea@marvelousmousetravels.com)

Queens, New York

Favorite Type of Butterbeer: Hot

Chelsea has been an agent since 2016. She loves the Wizarding World, and it is her favorite part of the parks. As a huge Harry Potter fan, she loves how incredibly th the parks are and how it feels like you have stepped into the pages of the books.

Quinn Lacy
(quinn@marvelousmousetravels.com)

Concord, North Carolina

Favorite Snack: Butterbeer

Quinn has been an agent since 2020. She is a Ravenclaw, and her favorite thing about the Wizarding World of Harry Potter are the awesome rides and cool experiences you can only enjoy at The Wizarding World of Harry Potter!

Brittany Lapicki
(brittany.lapicki@marvelousmousetravels.com)

Totowa, New Jersey

Favorite Ride: Hagrid's Magical Creatures Motorbike Adventure

Brittany has been an agent since September 2018. Her favorite thing about the Wizarding World of Harry Potter is the amazing attractions and all of the details throughout Diagon Alley and Hogsmeade.

Brenda "Tuk Tuk" Schruefer
(brenda.schruefer@marvelousmousetravels.com)
Fallston, Maryland

Favorite WWOHP Drink: Heavenly Hazelnut Milkshake

Brenda has been an agent since March 2018. Her favorite thing about the Wizarding World of Harry Potter is the Honeydukes candy store... It's amazing!

PREPARE FOR YOUR TRIP

TICKETS

In order to see and do it all, you will want to purchase "park-to-park" tickets. This type of ticket will allow you to visit both Islands of Adventure and Universal Studios Florida theme parks on the same day. The reason this is so important for you Wizards and Witches is because this type of ticket is <u>required</u> to ride the Hogwarts Express. If you do not have a "park-to-park" ticket, you will NOT be able to ride the Hogwarts Express. Each way you travel on the Hogwarts Express features a different "show" during your ride. It is also the only way to experience all of the Wizarding World in one day since the parks spans across both Universal Studios Orlando and Islands of Adventure. Even if you have multiple days planned at the theme parks, you want this type of ticket for flexibility and to completely immerse yourself into The Wizarding World of Harry Potter!

EXPRESS PASSES

Express Passes are also a great way to maximize your time in the WWOHP! There are two types of Express Passes: single use or unlimited. Single use Express Passes allow you to enter the ride queue's express lane only one time per participating attraction. Unlimited Express Passes allow you to enter the ride queue's express lane as many times as you desire per participating attraction! Don't want to wait in lines? Get Express Passes! It is as simple as that!

VIP TOURS

Are you a Wizard/Witch who wants to cast a spell that eliminates all waiting and takes you backstage at the Wizarding World? Maybe that spell could get you to the front of the line at Hagrid's Magical Creatures Motorbike Adventure? Then a VIP tour is for you! VIP tours can be booked as non-private or private; the primary difference is that in a private VIP tour, you get to create your own specific itinerary for the day!

EARLY PARK ADMISSION

Early Park Admission is a one-hour early admission benefit exclusive to onsite resort guests or guests that purchase their tickets through a qualified agency, like Marvelous Mouse Travels! This Early Park Admission benefit sometimes occurs at both parks or either park; the schedule is determined by Universal about a month in advance. No matter which park or parks are offering Early Park Admission, you will want to experience this! Want to get a photo in Diagon Alley with just you and the dragon? This is your chance!

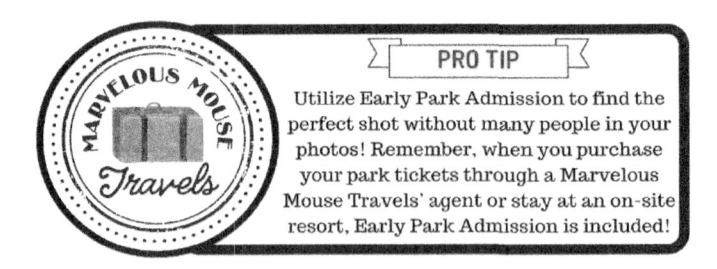

PRO TIP

Utilize Early Park Admission to find the perfect shot without many people in your photos! Remember, when you purchase your park tickets through a Marvelous Mouse Travels' agent or stay at an on-site resort, Early Park Admission is included!

THE EXCLUSIVE HARRY POTTER PACKAGE

If you are the ultimate Harry Potter fan, ask your Marvelous Mouse Travels' agent about booking you the Exclusive Harry Potter Vacation Package! This package includes hotel accommodations, tickets, breakfast at the Leaky Cauldron, breakfast at Three Broomsticks, a Shutterbutton's photo session, and a keepsake box with Harry Potter lanyards and luggage tags. There is a three-night minimum stay for this package.

For more information regarding tickets, express passes, Early Park Admission and other important details such as transportation, parking, and policies, purchase "A Marvelous Guide to Universal Orlando."

WIZARDING WORLD OF HARRY POTTER

Did you wait for a letter from Hogwarts on your 11th birthday? Always dreamed of boarding the Hogwarts Express on September 1st? Wanted to know what house you would be sorted into? You will feel right at home when you visit The Wizarding World of Harry Potter! A trip to the Wizarding World is a "must do" for any Harry Potter fan. The Wizarding World of Harry Potter (WWOHP) is spread out across both Islands of Adventure and Universal Studios Florida. Islands of Adventure features the wizarding village of Hogsmeade and Hogwarts Castle. This section was the first of the two Harry Potter lands to open. It opened on June 18, 2010 and has been a hit ever since. J.K. Rowling supervised the entire project with Stuart Craig, Production Designer for all eight films, and Alan Gilmore, Art Director for *Harry Potter and the Prisoner of Azkaban* and *Harry Potter and the Goblet of Fire*. Due to the popularity of this land, Universal Studios decided to open a second Harry Potter section, this time next door at Universal Studios Florida. Diagon Alley officially opened on July 8, 2014.

HOGSMEADE

Hogsmeade is nestled in between the Jurassic Park Island and the Lost Continent Island. We recommend entering from the Lost Continent side, as you will go through the Hogsmeade archway into the village before ending at Hogwarts Castle.

RIDES

Hogsmeade features four rides.

Hogwarts Express

Board the train and travel to King's Cross Station in London. On your journey, you may encounter some familiar events and characters from the books and films! The Hogwarts Express requires a park-to-park ticket to ride. It will take you from the village of Hogsmeade to King's Cross Station, just outside the entrance of Diagon Alley. Upon boarding, you will be directed to a car; each car seats up to eight people. As you journey to Diagon Alley, be sure to keep an eye out for some magical friends and "Easter eggs."

- Height Requirement- Under 48" (122 cm), supervising companion required
- Express Pass accepted
- Child Swap- Not Available
- Single Rider Line- Not Available
- Locker not required. Medical Detector not required.
- Accessibility and Restrictions- Wheelchair accessible; ECV accessible; Service Animal rest area

Hagrid's Magical Creature Motorbike Adventure

Hagrid's is the newest and, arguably, most popular attraction in all of the Wizarding World! This is a thrilling rollercoaster adventure through the Forbidden Forest and beyond on Hagrid's (previously Sirius') enchanted motorbike! You can choose to sit on the motorbike or in the sidecar. There are test seats available at the ride's entrance, so you can make sure you will be comfortable.

Please note, for this attraction, there is sometimes (primarily during peak seasons) a virtual queue that you can enter by scanning the QR codes located on signs throughout the parks or by visiting vlest.universalorlando.com.

- Height Requirement- Minimum 48" (122 cm)
- Express Pass not accepted
- Child Swap- Available
- Single Rider Line- Available
- Ride Photo Opportunity
- Locker required. Metal Detector not required.
- Accessibility and Restrictions- Guests must transfer from wheelchair; Test seating available at attraction entrance

> **PRO TIP**
>
> Buy your tickets from a Marvelous Mouse Travel to receive the Early Park Admission benefit! Some of the rides available in Hogsmeade for Early Park Admission are:
> Flight of the Hippogriff
> Harry Potter and the Forbidden Journey
> Hagrid's Magical Creatures Motorbike Adventure

Flight of the Hippogriff

If Hagrid's is a little too thrilling for you, you can try the Flight of the Hippogriff. This attraction is a family-friendly rollercoaster that swoops around the pumpkin patch and Hagrid's hut.

- Height Requirement- Minimum 36" (91 cm)
- Express Pass accepted
- Child Swap- Available
- Single Rider Line- Not Available
- Locker not required. Metal Detector not required.
- Accessibility and Restrictions- Guests must transfer from wheelchair

Harry Potter and the Forbidden Journey

This ride is inside Hogwarts Castle and takes you on a journey throughout Hogwarts, the castle grounds, and beyond! This is a thrilling ride that features a KUKA robotic arm that will tilt, dive, and pivot your row of four as it moves along the track. If you are prone to motion sickness, you may want to sit this one out.

- Height Requirement- Minimum 48" (122 cm)
- Express Pass accepted
- Child Swap- Available
- Single Rider Line- Available
- Ride Photo Opportunity
- Locker required. Metal Detector not required.
- Accessibility and Restrictions- Guests must transfer from wheelchair; Test seating available at attraction entrance

If you cannot or would rather not ride, you can still explore Hogwarts! Just ask for a tour of the castle! You will be able to walk throughout the queue which features iconic rooms such as the Defense Against the Dark Arts classroom, Dumbledore's office (no password needed!), and hallways featuring the Fat Lady portrait, portraits of all four Hogwarts' founders, and the sorting hat!

ADDITIONAL RIDE INFORMATION

Guests whose waistline is at least 40" (102 cm) or greater may not be accommodated on the following rides and are encouraged to try the test seat provided at the ride entrance:

- Hagrid's Magical Creatures Motorbike Adventure
- Harry Potter and the Forbidden Journey
- Flight of the Hippogriff

Fun Fact

Harry Potter and the Forbidden Journey uses cutting edge technology that had just been introduced to the theme park industry. Using a KUKA Arm (typically used to assemble vehicles) to hold the bench from above, the bench seamlessly pivots between scenes, creating the illusion of flying.

ENTERTAINMENT

As far as entertainment, you will not be disappointed! There is a stage between Hogsmeade and Hogwarts Castle that is home to two fantastic shows, The Triwizard Spirit Rally and The Hogwarts Frog Choir. The Triwizard Spirit Rally features students from fellow wizarding schools, Beauxbatons and

Durmstrang, as they put on displays of martial arts and dancing. Afterwards, both sets of students are available for photos! The Hogwarts Frog Choir features four Hogwarts students and their frog companions singing some famous wizarding tunes. During the holiday season, they will also sing some seasonal favorites! Both the Triwizard Spirit Rally and Frog Choir play multiple times per day, so be sure to check out the most current schedule on The Official Universal Orlando App.

On select nights, Hogwarts Castle comes to life in a dazzling display of lights and music. All four houses are celebrated in the display, and it is not to be missed! The show has multiple viewing times per night, so be sure to check out the most current schedule to make sure you do not miss them. We recommend going to the latest showing because they are more beautiful at night. The viewing area does tend to get crowded, so we recommend arriving 10-15 minutes early or, again, waiting until the last showing. A great spot is right in front of the wizarding snowman.

Be sure to stop at the front of the Hogwarts Express where you will be able to converse and take pictures with the conductor! During the Halloween season, be on the lookout for roaming Death Eaters!

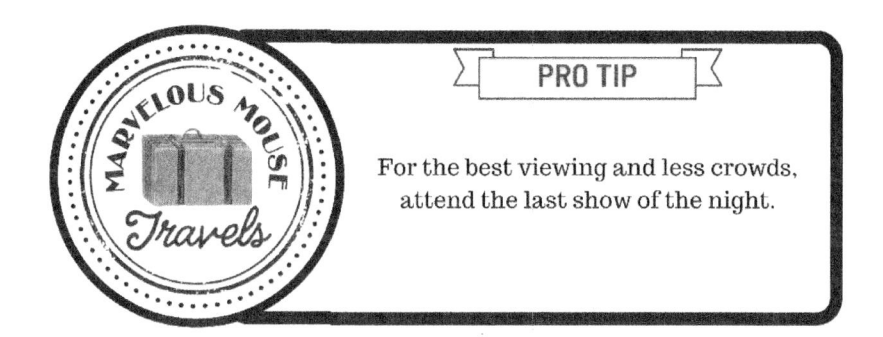

> **PRO TIP**
>
> For the best viewing and less crowds, attend the last show of the night.

SHOPPING

One of the best parts about taking a vacation is bringing home some awesome souvenirs to remember your trip... Let's take a look at the shops in Hogsmeade and some of the wizarding items you can bring back to the muggle world.

Filch's Emporium of Confiscated Goods

This shop is located in Hogwarts Castle and is located at the exit of Harry Potter and the Forbidden Journey. You can find Hogwarts' apparel, house-specific items, a set of wizarding chess, or even your very own copy of the Marauders Map! This is also where you will be able to view and purchase your ride photo so definitely make sure you stop!

Dervish and Banges, Owl Post & Owlery, and Ollivanders

All three shops are connected, and you can purchase wands (interactive and non-interactive), stationary, house robes, and even personalized quidditch jerseys. At Ollivanders you can experience your very own wand-selection ceremony! After the ceremony at Ollivanders, you will be escorted into these connected shops. In the Owlery section, you can send out actual mail (from postcards to packages) that will be stamped with a

Hogsmeade postmark. (This is great for sending holiday or birthday cards to Harry Potter fans!)

> **PRO TIP**
> The owl post is a fully functional post office! You can purchase stationary, postcards, and then mail them with a special Hogsmeade postmark!

Honeydukes

In this shop, you will find all of the sweets and treats you wished you could eat while reading the books and watching the movies. You can stock up on chocolate frogs (including collectible cards), Bertie Bott's Every Flavour Beans (they really are "every flavor," so be careful which ones you choose!), Fizzing Whizbees, Pepper Imps, Lemon Drops (Dumbledore's favorite and the password to his office), and so much more! Speaking of treats, let's talk about all the delicious food options here in Hogsmeade!

DINING

There is one quick service restaurant, The Three Broomsticks, inside Hogsmeade. Connected to this restaurant is the Hog's Head pub. Hogsmeade also has several snack and Butterbeer carts through the area.

The Three Broomsticks

You will feel just like a Hogwarts student when you eat at the Three Broomsticks. It features some delicious meals such as the Great Feast Platter for four and, of course, serves up Butterbeer.

In fact, you can get five of the six types of Butterbeer at The Three Broomsticks: Frozen, Cold, Hot, Ice Cream or Potted Cream! There is both an indoor and outdoor seating area. The indoor area is incredibly themed. Outside, you can grab a seat with an amazing view of Hogwarts Castle. The Three Broomsticks is open for breakfast, lunch, and dinner, but you will need a voucher/reservation for breakfast. This advanced reservation can be added to a vacation package of three or more nights or will be included with the Exclusive Harry Potter Vacation Package.

Menu Options: Fish and Chips, Shepherd's Pie, Rotisserie Chicken, Ribs, Turkey Legs, and Butterbeer.

Quick Service dining available.

Price Range- $14.99 and under per adult

Fan Favorite- **The Great Feast** (platter serves four)- The first course is a fresh garden salad tossed with a vinaigrette dressing. The main course is a combination of rotisserie smoked chicken and spareribs served with corn on the cob and roasted potatoes.

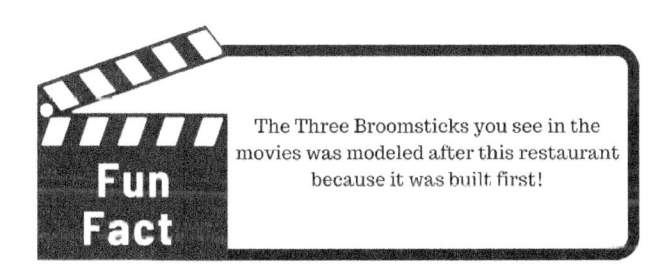

Fun Fact: The Three Broomsticks you see in the movies was modeled after this restaurant because it was built first!

Hog's Head

The Hog's Head pub is located right next door to The Three Broomsticks. This is where you can grab a Butterbeer, pumpkin juice, or an alcoholic beverage such as a Dragon Scale Lager or Wizard's Brew Stout. You can even get something off a secret menu... Just ask your bartender for a special mix!

Menu Options: Butterbeer, Pumpkin Juice, alcoholic, and non-alcoholic beverages.

Casual Dining available.

Price Range- $8 and under per menu item

Fan Favorite- **Hog's Tea-** Hogsmeade's version of a Long Island Iced Tea

> **PRO TIP**
> Visit Hog's Head for a butterbeer instead of waiting in the long line at the butterbeer cart!

Butterbeer Cart

There is a Butterbeer cart located across from Hogwarts Castle where you can grab a refreshing Butterbeer (cold or frozen), pumpkin juice, lemonade, gilly water, or sweet tea.

ANNUAL EVENTS

Dark Arts at Hogwarts Castle

The Dark Arts at Hogwarts Castle projection show runs from dusk to park close and features Lord Voldemort, dementors, and more! This foreboding projection show is the perfect way to ring in the spooky season in Hogsmeade.

During the Halloween season (typically starting mid-September), the streets of Hogsmeade will be tinted an ominous shade of green and Death Eaters will be roaming! Keep your wand ready, as they may just try to duel you if they do not see your dark mark.

The Magic of Christmas at Hogwarts Castle
Similar to The Nighttime Lights at Hogwarts Castle, this family-friendly nighttime show features holiday-themed projections on Hogwarts Castle. Watch in awe as colorful lights, jovial music, and various character projections light up the Castle at night. The nine-minute show is pure magic and a must for all ages!

Christmas in The Wizarding World of Harry Potter- Hogsmeade
Enjoy festive decor, lights, and music (check out the Frog Choir's Christmas concert) in Hogsmeade, as you sip on holiday drinks and eat delicious food. Be sure to stay for The Magic of Christmas at Hogwarts Castle nighttime entertainment at the conclusion of your night. For the least crowded viewing, watch the last show of the night!

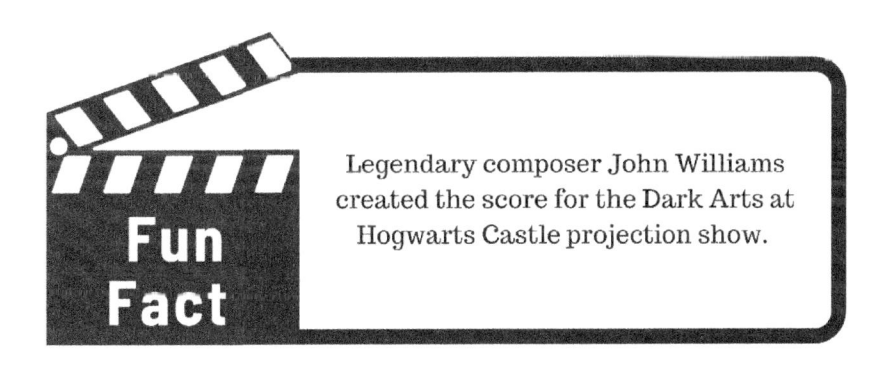

Fun Fact: Legendary composer John Williams created the score for the Dark Arts at Hogwarts Castle projection show.

DIAGON ALLEY

Diagon Alley is well-hidden from muggles in Universal Studios Florida. It is located in the former Amity area where the Jaws attraction was housed. You will notice traces of magic before you even enter Diagon Alley. On the memorable London Street, you will find 12 Grimmauld Place and the Knight Bus. Although this section of the WWOHP only has one ride, there is still plenty to experience, as it is the most immersive area from both parks.

RIDES

Harry Potter and the Escape from Gringotts

Harry Potter and the Escape from Gringotts is a multi-sensory 3D thrill ride. It puts you in the middle of the action from *Harry Potter and the Deathly Hallows*. Harry, Ron, and Hermione have broken into Gringotts and now must escape! This ride is full of twists and turns, Death Eaters, and even a dragon! There are test seats available at the ride's entrance, so you can make sure you will be comfortable. If you are unable or do not want to ride, you can still tour Gringotts just like Hogwarts Castle! Just ask a ride team member if you can take a tour of the bank.

- Height Requirement- Minimum Height 42" (101.6 cm). Under 48" (121.9 cm), supervising companion required
- Express Pass accepted
- Child Swap- Available
- Single Rider Line- Available
- Queue Photo Opportunity
- Locker required. Medical Detector not required.
- Accessibility and Restrictions- Guests must transfer from wheelchair; Guests must secure or remove prosthetic limbs; Test seating available at attraction entrance

Hogwarts Express

The Hogwarts Express is located outside Diagon Alley on London Street and requires a park-to-park ticket to ride. We can't give too much away, but someone will be waiting for you on the other side. It will take you from King's Cross Station to Hogsmeade Station in Islands of Adventure. There is a great photo/video opportunity in the queue line of the ride! You will actually "disappear" through the wall between platforms 9 and 10 to make it onto platform 9 ¾. Upon boarding, you will be directed to a car; each car seats up to eight people.

- Height Requirement- Under 48" (121.9 cm), supervising companion required
- Express Pass accepted
- Child Swap- Not Available
- Single Rider Line- Not Available
- Locker not required. Medical Detector not required.
- Accessibility and Restrictions- Wheelchair accessible; ECV accessible; Service Animal rest area

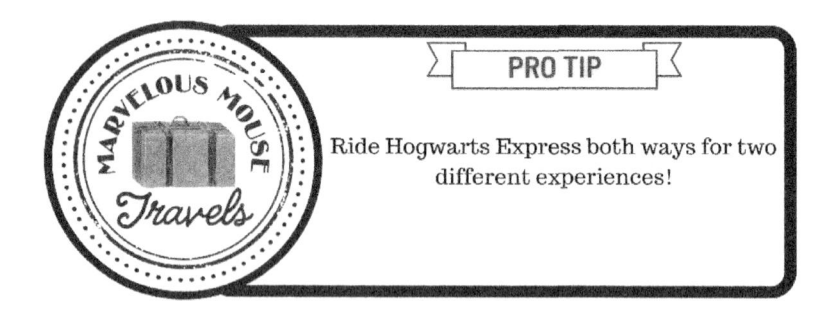

PRO TIP

Ride Hogwarts Express both ways for two different experiences!

ADDITIONAL RIDE INFORMATION

Guests whose waistline is at least 40" (102 cm) or greater may not be accommodated on the following rides and are encouraged to try the test seat provided at the ride entrance:

- Harry Potter and the Escape from Gringotts

ENTERTAINMENT

There is plenty to keep you entertained while wandering around this part of the WWOHP. Outside on the streets of London, you can visit the Knight Bus, the emergency transport for stranded witches or wizards. This is an actual prop from *Harry Potter and the Prisoner of Azkaban*! Here, you can interact with the conductor and the shrunken head driver. Be sure to head around to the back of the bus to peek inside!

Along this street, you will also find 12 Grimmauld Place, the Black family home. Keep an eye on the second-floor windows... You may just see a certain surly house elf peeking out from behind the curtains.

Before you head through the magical brick wall and into Diagon Alley, make a stop at the red phone booth. Be connected to the Ministry of Magic by dialing "MAGIC!"

Once inside, you can catch some live shows! There is a stage in the Carkitt Market where you can see The Tales of Beedle the Bard, a performance by four students from the Wizarding Academy of Dramatic Arts, or a performance by Molly Weasley's favorite singer, Celestina Warbeck and the Banshees. Both are not to be missed!

At the Gringotts Money Exchange, you can not only change your muggle money for some knuts and galleons, but you can also interact with one of the Gringotts goblins. Here, you are allowed to exchange your U.S. currency for Gringotts' bank notes, which can be used in Diagon Alley, Hogsmeade, and various locations throughout the theme parks. Only $10 and $20 denominations are accepted. Definitely stop in and say hello!

Just like in Hogsmeade, you can enjoy the show at Ollivanders and hope you are the lucky witch or wizard the wand chooses! This location has two show rooms, though, so the line tends to move quicker than the one located in Hogsmeade.

SHOPPING

Just like in the books and movies, Diagon Alley is known for its shopping! Here you will find everything you need for the Wizarding World.

Weasleys' Wizard Wheezes

You will find everything you need to cause chaos at Hogwarts in Fred and George Weasley's joke shop! You will be able to purchase some of their original creations such as skiving snackboxes, decoy detonators, and you can even adopt a Pygmy Puff! While muggle visitors can only access the first floor, make sure you look up once inside. There are fireworks on the ceiling, and you can see some of their other products from the books/movies such as Peruvian instant darkness powder.

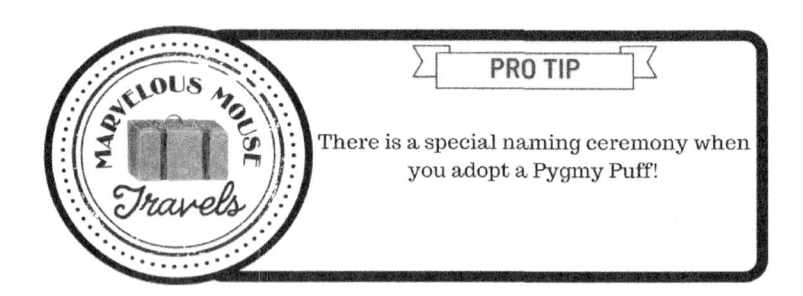

> **PRO TIP**
> There is a special naming ceremony when you adopt a Pygmy Puff!

Quality Quidditch Supplies

All quidditch fans need to be sure to stop in here! You can purchase brooms, quidditch balls, your house quidditch apparel, and even custom quidditch jerseys.

Sugarplum's Sweetshop

Similar to Honeydukes in Hogsmeade, you can find all of your favorite wizarding sweets and treats here such as cauldron cakes and chocolate frogs. Sugarplum's also connects inside to both Quality Quidditch Supplies and Weasley's Wizard Wheezes.

Wands by Gregorovitch

You can purchase an interactive or non-interactive wand at this cart located across from Weasley's Wizard Wheezes with little to no wait!

Globus Mundi
Even wizards use travel agents! Stop in at this wizarding travel agency to get everything you will need for your travels. Check out the windows for some amazing travel deals available to witches and wizards.

Gringotts Money Exchange
You can exchange your muggle money for wizarding money to use throughout the parks or keep as a souvenir. This is also where you will be able to interact with a Gringott's goblin.

Scribbulus
Get all of your school and office essentials here such as parchment, ink, quills, notebooks, wax seals, and backpacks.

Wiseacre's Wizarding Equipment
You can find an assortment of Wizarding World items including Butterbeer-themed merchandise.

Madam Malkin's Robes for All Occasions
You will find everything you need for the wizarding section of your wardrobe at Madam Malkin's! You will be able to purchase house robes, sweaters made by Molly Weasley, accessories, and even replica jewelry and outfits straight from the movies. Don't forget to try things on in front of the mirror... It may just give you its opinion!

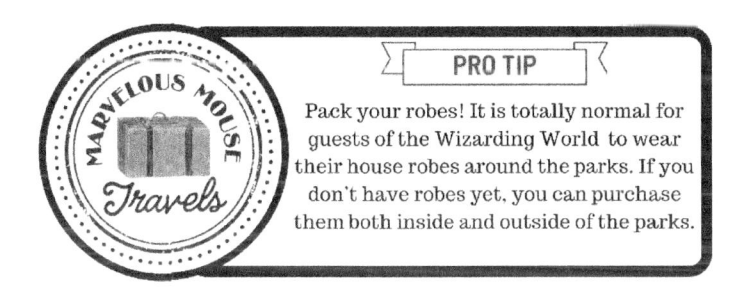

PRO TIP

Pack your robes! It is totally normal for guests of the Wizarding World to wear their house robes around the parks. If you don't have robes yet, you can purchase them both inside and outside of the parks.

Ollivanders
You can choose from interactive and non-interactive wands, wands used by your favorite characters, and the current year's limited-edition wand. If you want something unique, chat with one of the wandmakers who can help you choose a wand based on your birthday.

Shutterbutton's Photography Studio
Have you ever wished you could have a wizarding moving picture? Now you can! Just book a session at Shutterbutton's! With a little magic, you will be able to walk away with a CD album full of moving pictures. This is included with the Exclusive Harry Potter Vacation Package. Reservations are first-come, first-served unless you have booked the Exclusive Harry Potter Vacation Package; this package allows guests to make a reservation in advance.

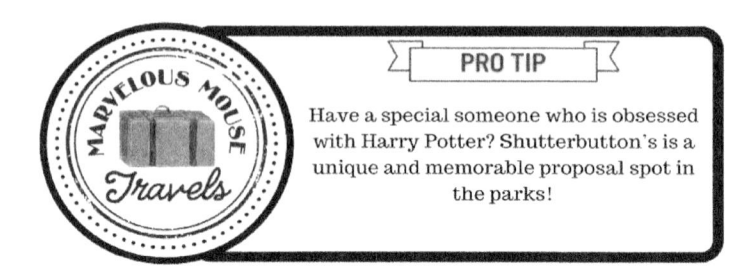

> **PRO TIP**
> Have a special someone who is obsessed with Harry Potter? Shutterbutton's is a unique and memorable proposal spot in the parks!

Magical Menagerie
Every witch and wizard needs a magical pet. The Menagerie is where you can purchase owls, Pygmy Puffs, your very own Fang or Buckbeak, and more! Make sure you check out the side window where you will find a giant snake that you can practice your Parseltongue with.

Borgin and Burkes
Don't forget to venture down Knockturn Alley, so you can shop at Borgin and Burkes. This shop is infamous for catering

to dark witches and wizards. You can purchase death eater masks, wanted posters, death eater apparel, and more. In the back right of the store, you will spot something familiar from *Harry Potter and the Half Blood Prince-* a replica of the vanishing cabinet Draco used to sneak death eaters into Hogwarts.

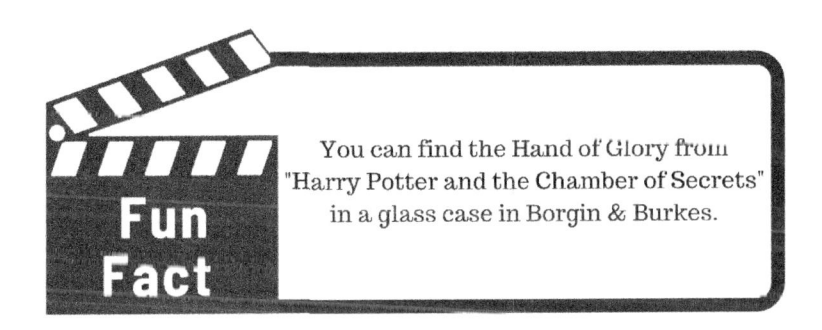

> **Fun Fact:** You can find the Hand of Glory from "Harry Potter and the Chamber of Secrets" in a glass case in Borgin & Burkes.

DINING

After all that shopping, you are bound to have worked up an appetite!

Leaky Cauldron

Stop into the Leaky Cauldron to dine on traditional English meals! Outside, watch out if you stand under the sign… The cauldron really leaks! Looking for Butterbeer in Diagon Alley? Here, you can order four of the six types: Cold, Frozen, Hot, and Potted Cream! Leaky Cauldron is open for breakfast, lunch, and dinner, but you will need a voucher/reservation for breakfast. This advanced reservation can be added to a vacation package of three or more nights or will be included with the Exclusive Harry Potter Vacation Package.

Menu Options: Fisherman's Pie, Toad in the Hole, Bangers and Mash, Ploughman's Platters, and Butterbeer.
Quick Service dining available.

Price Range- $14.99 and under per adult
Fan Favorite- Traditional Breakfast- Fresh scrambled eggs, sausage links, black pudding, English bacon, baked beans, grilled tomato, sautéed mushrooms, and breakfast potatoes.

Florean Fortescue's Ice-Cream Parlour

Florean Fortescue's is full of interesting ice cream flavors, and the perfect spot to cool off on a hot day! Definitely keep an open mind and try out some of the more unusual flavors such as Earl Grey & Lavender or Chocolate Chili! They also have Butterbeer ice cream.

Menu Options: Scoop and Soft Serve Ice Cream in flavors such as Butterbeer, Earl Grey and Lavender, Chocolate Chili, and many more. Serving bottled pumpkin juice, ciders, teas, and water.
Quick Service dining available.
Price Range- $14.99 and under per adult
Fan Favorite- Butterbeer Ice Cream- Butterbeer-flavored ice cream served in a waffle cone.

The Hopping Pot

You can purchase both alcoholic and non-alcoholic drinks, chips, beef pasties, and Butterbeer ice cream at this walk-up kiosk. This spot is perfect for grabbing something quick before catching one of the shows in Carkitt Market.

Menu Options: Butterbeer Ice Cream, Peachtree Fizzing Tea, Fishy Green Ale, and Various Brews
Quick Service dining available,
Price Range- $14.99 and under per adult
Fan Favorite- Beef Pastry- Savory pastry

The Fountain of Fair Fortune

The Fountain of Fair Fortune is named after one of the stories in the Tales of Beedle the Bard and serves up delicious beverages.

You can order an ice cold Butterbeer, pumpkin juice, or even a Dragon Scale beer. This location also serves hot Butterbeer seasonally.

Menu Options: Butterbeer, Frozen Butterbeer, Gillywater, Fishy Green Ale, Pumpkin Juice, and Otter's Fizzy Orange Juice
Quick Service dining available
Price Range- $14.99 and under per adult
Fan Favorite- **Pumpkin Juice**

Eternelle's Elixir of Refreshment

Choose a flavored Elixir such as Fire Protection Potion or Draught of Peace as an add-in to enhance your Gilly Water! This stand is located inside Carkitt Market across from the Gringotts Money Exchange.

WAND GUIDE

Wands are a great souvenir from your time in the Wizarding World. There are non-interactive and interactive wands. Standard, non-interactive wands have a white label and cost $55 (plus tax). The interactive wands allow you to cast spells across the Wizarding World, have a gold foil label, and cost $59 (plus tax). Each interactive wand comes with a map showing all of the different spell locations inside both Diagon Alley and Hogsmeade. Each spell location is marked with a gold medallion. If you need help casting a spell, there are witches and wizards available around each location to help. The secret spell locations will not be marked.

WAND SETS

There are several wand sets available for purchase.

Dumbledore's Army Set includes Harry, Ron, Hermione, Ginny, Neville, and Luna on a parchment-style display stand. This wand set costs $200 (plus tax) and is non-interactive.

The Triwizard Champions Set includes Harry, Cedric, Fleur, and Viktor on a display stand with the Triwizard Tournament logo. This wand set costs $160 (plus tax) and is non-interactive.

The Weasley Wand Set includes Fred and George on a display stand with Weasley Wizard Wheezes "W" accents. This wand set costs $100 and is non-interactive.

Wand	Interactive	Standard	Wand	Interactive	Standard
Harry Potter	✓	✓	Hermione	✓	✓
Ron Weasley	✓	✓	Dumbledore (Elder Wand)	✓	✓
Luna Lovegood	✓	✓	Neville Longbottom	✓	
Fred Weasley	✓	✓	George Weasley	✓	✓
Ginny Weasley	✓	✓	Molly Weasley		✓
Arthur Weasley		✓	Fleur Delacour	✓	✓
Cho Chang	✓	✓	Cedric Diggory	✓	✓
Viktor Krum		✓	Professor McGonagall	✓	✓
Professor Slughorn		✓	Mad Eye Moody	✓	
Remus Lupin	✓		Nymphadora Tonks	✓	
Sirius Black	✓		Xenophilius Lovegood		✓
Rufus Scrimgeour					
Professor Snape	✓	✓	Narcissa Malfoy	✓	✓
Draco Malfoy	✓	✓	Lucius Malfoy	✓	✓
Lord Voldemort	✓	✓	Bellatrix Lestrange	✓	✓
Yaxley	✓	✓	Peter Pettigrew	✓	
Death Eater Snake	✓	✓	Death Eater Swirl	✓	✓
Death Eater Thorns		✓	Death Eater Skull		✓
Newt Scamander	✓	✓	Leta Lestrange	✓	✓
Queenie Goldstein	✓	✓	Seraphina Picquery	✓	✓
Albus Dumbledore	✓	✓	Theseus Scamander		✓
Gellert Grindlewald		✓	Nicholas Flamel	✓	
2022 Collectors Wand	✓		Holly Wood*	✓	
Alder Wood*	✓		Ivy Wood*	✓	
Ash Wood*	✓		Oak Wood*	✓	
Birch Wood*	✓		Reed Wood*	✓	
Elder Wood*	✓		Rowan Wood*	✓	
Hawthorn Wood*	✓		Vine Wood*	✓	
Hazel Wood*	✓				

*based on celtic calendar and corresponds to specific dates

COLLECTIBLE WAND

Every year a special collector's wand is released retailing at $75 (plus tax).

WAND STAND

Need somewhere special to display your wand when you are in the muggle world? You can choose from different styles to match your wand or wands!

Post a pic and let us know which was your favorite in our Universal Facebook Group- **Universal Studios Orlando Deals, Planning, & Tips!**

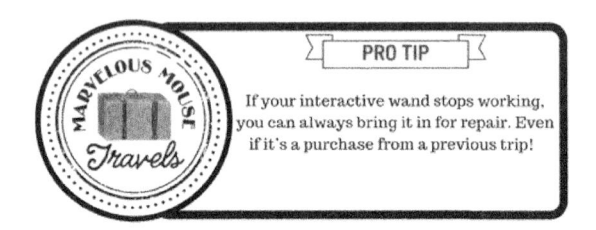

PRO TIP

If your interactive wand stops working, you can always bring it in for repair. Even if it's a purchase from a previous trip!

SECRETS

LONDON

In London, there are tributes to the former Jaws attraction, which sat on the same site as Diagon Alley and closed in 2012 after 22 years. You can find one of these tributes in the London waterfront area in the window of a record store. There is a record titled "Here's to Swimmin' with Bow-Legged Women" by the Quint Trio displayed here. This references a toast made by Quint, a shark hunter in the Spielberg blockbuster.

Kreacher, the grumpy Black family house elf, can be spotted in a window of the Blacks' home at 12 Grimmauld Place. Keep an eye on the windows, and you will see him peering out every so often.

The traditional red phone booth outside King's Cross isn't just for show. If you dial 62442 (MAGIC) using the phone, you will be connected to the Ministry of Magic.

The Knight Bus at Universal Studios Florida is one of the two authentic prop buses used in the movie, *Harry Potter and the Prisoner of Azkaban*.

DIAGON ALLEY

Magical Menagerie

The mythical Crumple-Horned Snorkack, beloved by Luna Lovegood, can be spotted on the second level of the Magical Menagerie store.

On the side window, you will find a snake that will speak to you in Parseltongue and English.

Weasley's Wizard Wheezes

There are many secret finds in Weasley's Wizard Wheezes. Look up at the skylight, and you will see a perpetual fireworks display. You will also spot Peruvian Instant Darkness Powder; you may recognize this from *Harry Potter and the Half-Blood Prince* when Harry uses it to sneak into Draco Malfoy's train compartment.

On the second level, you can also find Umbridge balancing weights on a unicycle.

You can even participate in the Pygmy Puff naming ceremony; name it, ring the bell, and announce it through the store.

Ollivanders

The windows of this branch of Ollivanders are filled with some incredible details such as dragon heartstrings, Phoenix feathers, and unicorn hairs- all essential items to create wands. Harry Potter and Voldemort's wands have cores made of phoenix feathers from the same bird. Hermione's wand has a core made of dragon heartstring, and Ron's wand has a unicorn hair core.

Quality Quidditch Supplies

Take a look at the windows above the Quality Quidditch Supplies store. Pennants from the teams seen in the movies including Puddlemere United, the Chudley Cannons, the Montrose Magpies, and the Holyhead Harpies are featured.

The Quidditch trophies from the movie sets are also kept on the top shelves.

Leaky Cauldron

The sign on the front of the Leaky Cauldron restaurant actually leaks water!

The luggage inside is also from the films!

Madam Malkin's Robes for All Occasions

Madame Malkin's sells the finest robes for all your wizarding occasions including jewelry, Mrs. Weasley's famous sweaters, and replicas of Hermione's Yule Ball gown and Dumbledore's robes. Not sure if the robe you picked is "the one?" Just ask the talking mirror.

Dervish and Banges

Dervish and Banges, known for their array of magical items such as Sneakoscopes, Spectrespecs, and Omnioculars, also has quite the Quidditch line. From Quaffles, Golden Snitches, and browns (even the Nimbus Two Thousand and One and the Firebolt!) to clothing such as uniforms, robes, scarves, ties, and t-shirts, there is something in here for all Quidditch fans.

If you happen to see the Monster Book of Monsters, watch your fingers! This book snaps, growls, and even charges at people as they pass by!

Carkitt Market

Inside Carkitt Market, try asking the animatronic goblin in the Gringotts Money Exchange if he is a house elf and see what response you get!

Wiseacre's Wizarding Equipment

In Wiseacre's Wizarding Equipment, sitting on Bill Weasley's desk is the microscope that Bill uses in the pre-show portion of *Harry Potter and the Escape from Gringotts*.

The barometer was used twice in the Harry Potter films: in Dumbledore's office in *Harry Potter and the Half-Blood Prince* and in the Room of Requirement in *Harry Potter and the Deathly Hallows*.

Globus Mundi

After you have had a drink, something to eat, and watched a live show, you simply must stop by Globus Mundi. Don't let its small size fool you. This is the travel store for the "who's who" of witches and wizards, and there are some nice details tucked away inside.

Knockturn Alley

Knockturn Alley is the seedy corner of the Wizarding World. In the film, *Jaws*, Quint, Brody, and Hooper all sing "Show Me the Way to Go Home" while hunting down the deadly shark. As a homage to the ride that was previously located here, the shrunken heads in Knockturn Alley also perform this song.

Knockturn Alley is filled with black lights that will help you see the secret spells on your spells map.

Borgin and Burkes

If you listen closely to the Vanishing Cabinet in Borgin and Burkes, you will hear a bird chirping away inside.

On the second level of the store, 90% of the props and set dressings are actually from the Harry Potter films.

King's Cross

The bench on Platform 9¾ and the luggage racks inside the Hogwarts Express are actual props from the movies!

Ultimately, Universal accepted that guests passing through a wall was not actually practical. So, to the benefit of waiting riders, they settled on using the Pepper's Ghost technique; this neat effect dates back to the nineteenth century. A sheet of glass was built into a large luggage cart sitting between those "walking through" the wall and those watching them. In conjunction with mirrors, lighting, and sound effects, this created the illusion of guests walking through the wall to guests behind in the queue. In reality, the guest simply walked through a zig-zag section of the queue. Add a sound effect indicating they passed onto the mythical platform, and the illusion has been successfully created! Now the guest is off to begin their magical journey to Hogwarts!

In King's Cross Station, you will see a perfume advertisement that looks very similar to the one Harry and Professor Dumbledore stand by in *Harry Potter and the Half-Blood Prince*.

If you pay close attention, you might recognize one passenger who is waiting on the King's Cross platform... Hedwig, Harry Potter's owl.

If you are waiting for a train, do not forget you are in Eastern Standard Time. The times on the train schedule correspond with real destinations and the actual time of day in the United Kingdom.

Harry Potter and the Escape from Gringotts
In the pre-show for the Gringotts' ride, look out for a moving picture frame showing the Weasley family in Egypt, seen in *Harry Potter and the Prisoner of Azkaban*.

The Gringotts' dragon breathes fire that is 3,560° Fahrenheit- more than 16 times hotter than boiling water!

The Gringotts' dragon breathes fire every 10 minutes on the zero. You know she is about to breathe fire when you hear her growl. However, she will not breathe fire if it is slightly windy in the area.

HOGSMEADE

Muggles nipping at your ankles? Hogsmeade Village is the only Muggle-Free settlement in all of Britain (no children permitted).

You can hear Moaning Myrtle in the bathroom next to Three Broomsticks Pub and Restaurant. While you are in there, keep an eye out for the house elves (watch for their shadows).

There is a secret menu at Hog's Head. You can get beer cocktails like a Black Hog (Black and Tan), Hog's Bite (Snakebite), or Triple (three kinds of beer). There are even cocktails like the Hog's Tea (Long Island Iced Tea), Pear Dazzle (pear cider, lemonade, vodka), and Apple Jack (apple cider, Jack Daniels, soda water).

Howlers are on display as holographic messages at the Owl Post. There are quite a few messages playing on rotation!

Between the Hogsmeade train platform and Hogsmeade Village, you will pass this easily overlooked horseless carriage pulled by trained thestrals, a dangerous animal that looks like a skeletal horse with bat wings. Every now and then, it leaps and shimmies. You cannot see the thestrals for yourself because you are not a wizard and have not suffered enough pain.

Zonkos Joke Shop

Zonkos is your destination for novelty items, jokes, and toys; it is the only place you can purchase portable swamps. Stop by Zonkos to pick up your own extendable ears, screaming yo-yos, Pygmy Puffs, and more. Magical sweet tooth? There are sweets including Fainting Fancies, Fever Fudge, Nosebleed Nougat, and U-No-Poo.

Hogsmeade Bookstore

Kenneth Branagh makes a cameo appearance as Gilderoy Lockhart in the window of the Hogsmeade Bookstore. He is surrounded by mockups of Lockhart's memoirs including *Travels with Trolls* and *A Year with a Yeti*.

Harry Potter and the Forbidden Journey

The line to get on to Harry Potter and the Forbidden Journey is just as amazing as the ride itself! You will pass by the Mirror of Erised, the Sorting Hat, paintings of the founders of Hogwarts conversing with each other (they are each holding items Voldemort turned into Horcruxes except Godric Gryffindor's sword), Dumbledore's Pensieve, an interactive Fat Lady portrait, Mandrakes, and the gargoyle that guards Dumbledore's office throughout the queue.

Filch's Emporium of Confiscated Goods

Missing a bone after Forbidden Journey? As you leave, there are a few bottles of Skele-Gro tucked away on shelves at Filch's Emporium of Confiscated Goods.

Look for the column filled with items he has confiscated from Hogwarts troublemakers!

Ask to be "sorted" by the Sorting Hat. The Sorting Hat will have a look inside your mind and tell you where you belong.

Hagrid's Magical Creatures Motorbike Adventure

Hagrid has been teaching for a long time, and the students in the Wizarding World have the same impulses as muggle kids. Hagrids' kids decorated the walls with graffiti including jokes about a hippogriff snatching Draco Malfoy and a heart with James and Lily's initials.

Hagrid has hung many cages from the ceiling of the graffiti-covered room. Though they may look empty, something periodically scampers through them, making all of the crates and nets rustle and chirp.

The animated Hagrid figure on the ride features an extensive motion profile of 24 different body movements and facial expressions, mimicking Robbie Coltrane's exact motions as Hagrid. Robbie Coltrane even recorded a custom script as Hagrid for the ride. Also, the height of the animated figure is 7 feet 6 inches tall, exactly proportional to Hagrid in the Harry Potter film series.

A digital scan of Robbie Coltrane's mouth was used to create Hagrid's teeth. Hagrid's entire face was meticulously sculpted by hand, and Hagrid's costume was designed by the same team that created his on-screen wardrobe.

Flight of the Hippogriff

Flight of the Hippogriff is on the grounds of Hagrid's hut where you can hear Fang barking. Also listen for Hagrid giving you instructions on the proper way to approach a Hippogriff as you board the ride.

BUTTERBEER

Arguably, the most popular food or drink associated with the Wizarding World is Butterbeer! Butterbeer first appeared in *Harry Potter and the Prisoner of Azkaban* where Harry tried it and said it was the most delicious thing he had ever tasted and seemed to heat every bit of him from the inside. Once you try it for yourself, we are sure you will agree!

Butterbeer comes in six different forms in the Wizarding World - Hot, Cold, Frozen, Ice Cream, Potted Cream, and Fudge. You can find all six in both Diagon Alley and Hogsmeade. Due to popular demand, Hot Butterbeer is no longer seasonal and is now available year-round! Most people have a pretty strong opinion about which Butterbeer is best. We think the only way to find out is to try them all! Here is a guide to show you where you can get each type of Butterbeer plus some space for your ranking!

Type of Butterbeer	Where to Find it	Ranking
Cold Butterbeer "Regular"	Leaky Cauldron, The Hopping Pot, Three Broomsticks, Hog's Head, Butterbeer Carts	__ of 6
Frozen Butterbeer	Leaky Cauldron, The Hopping Pot, Three Broomsticks, Hog's Head, Butterbeer Carts	__ of 6
Hot Butterbeer	Leaky Cauldron, Three Broomsticks	__ of 6
Butterbeer Potted Cream	Leaky Cauldron, Three Broomsticks	__ of 6
Butterbeer Fudge	Sugarplum's Sweetshop, Honeydukes	__ of 6
Butterbeer Soft Serve Ice Cream	Florean Fortescue's Ice-Cream Parlor, The Hopping Pot, Three Broomsticks	__ of 6

RECIPE

You can even turn your Butterbeer beverage into a souvenir by ordering it in a souvenir mug! This is perfect for drinking your own homemade version once you return from your trip!

Check out this recipe to make your own, or you can order the Starbucks version also listed below:

Ingredients:

- 2 liters cream soda, chilled
- ¼ tsp caramel extract
- ¼ tsp butter extract

For the Cream Topping:

- 1 cup heavy whipping cream
- ½ cup butterscotch topping
- ¼ cup powdered sugar

Instructions:

1. In large mixing bowl, whip the heavy cream until it forms stiff peaks.
2. Add the butterscotch topping and powdered sugar.
3. Mix the caramel and butter extracts with the cream soda and pour the mixture into clear cups or mugs.
4. Top with the butterscotch cream topping and enjoy!

https://www.favfamilyrecipes.com/Butterbeer/

Starbucks Hot Butterbeer Latte Order:

- Whole milk steamer

- Add caramel syrup (2 for tall, 3 for grande, 4 for venti)

- Add toffee nut syrup (2 for tall, 3 for grande, 4 for venti)

- Add cinnamon dolce syrup (2 for tall, 3 for grande, 4 for venti)

- Whipped cream and salted caramel bits on top (or creme brulee topping, if you prefer)

- Optional if you prefer to add a coffee taste: Add a shot of espresso (2 for a grande or venti)

https://starbuckssecretmenu.net/starbucks-secret-menu-hot-Butterbeer-latte/

BUTTERBEER TIPS AND FUN FACTS

- If there is a long line for the Butterbeer Cart in Hogsmeade, you can head into Hogs Head which usually has little to no wait!

- Want to add a little caffeine boost? Grab a shot or two of espresso at Starbucks before heading to the Wizarding World and add it to your Butterbeer.

- The back of the Butterbeer Cart makes for a great picture backdrop!

- In the books, Luna Lovegood often wore a necklace made of Butterbeer corks.

- J.K. Rowling approved the secret recipe created by Ric Florell and Steve Jayson.

- If you really love Butterbeer, there is Butterbeer-themed merchandise for sale in both Hogsmeade and Diagon Alley.

- Winky the House Elf started to overindulge in Butterbeer after being fired by Mr. Crouch.

Fun Fact: A thousand free Butterbeer were given away in December of 2012 when the parks had hit 5 million glasses of Butterbeer served!

THE WIZARDING WORLD OF HARRY POTTER, 1-DAY 2-PARK ITINERARY

For the Harry Potter fans, have you ever wondered the best way to conquer both Hogsmeade in Islands of Adventure and Diagon Alley in Universal Studios Florida in one day? Marvelous Mouse Travels has you covered! The itinerary below is one of many ways you can enjoy both worlds.

To experience this plan, take advantage of Early Park Admission at Universal Studios Florida. As a reminder, all guests staying at on-site resorts receive Early Park Admission. Guests staying off-site who purchase tickets through Marvelous Mouse Travels will also receive this benefit.

Please note, to follow this sample itinerary, you will need to have park-to-park tickets. We also strongly recommend using Express Passes for the rides.

Let's get started...

The night before your adventure, make sure to check the Early Park Admission hours on The Official Universal Orlando App. If you have not already, pick up your tickets in advance at your resort's Universal Orlando Vacation Planning Center. This will save you time in the morning!

At the start of your day, enjoy an early breakfast at your resort.

Take advantage of Early Park Admission at Universal Studios Florida. We suggest being at the park entrance at least 30-45 minutes prior to opening.

Head straight to the streets of London and through the brick wall between Leicester Square Station and Wyndhams to Diagon Alley.

This is the time to take pictures inside Diagon Alley with the Gringott's Bank dragon behind you! Listen for the growl… It means she is about to spew fire, making an awesome photo opportunity for you!

Ride Harry Potter and the Escape from Gringotts. If you have a bag, you will have to use the ride lockers before you enter!

Join the virtual line for Hagrid's Magical Creatures Motorbike Adventure by visiting vltest.universalorlando.com. You will be prompted to enter the number of guests in your party and create an account with your email address. You can then choose Hagrid's as your ride and an available time. We recommend an afternoon time, if possible, since Hagrid's is located in Islands of Adventure. *Please note, Universal Studios only tests this virtual line system during peak seasons; it may not always be available, in which, you will have to use the standby line once inside Islands of Adventure.*

Every witch and wizard needs a wand, so be sure to stop at Ollivanders to get yours! You can then begin casting spells throughout the Wizarding World!

Head back outside to the streets of London (don't worry, you will be back) and go to King's Cross Station. Hop aboard the Hogwarts Express for a ride to the village of Hogsmeade in Islands of Adventure. You will need a park-to-park ticket to ride!

It is now time to explore Hogwarts! As you are in line for Harry Potter and the Forbidden Journey, enjoy all of the unique rooms and characters inside the castle!

At the ride exit, walk right over to Flight of the Hippogriff.

After all those rides, you are sure to have worked up an appetite! Grab a delicious lunch at the Three Broomsticks. We recommend the Shepherd's Pie with a side of pumpkin juice!

Explore the different shops and mail some postcards from the Owl Post.

Don't forget to head to Hagrid's when it is your turn to ride! There are some fun easter eggs in the queue as well, so keep an eye out for those!

Before heading back to Diagon Alley, be sure to check show times for the Triwizard Spirit Rally and Frog Choir shows! The show times are available in The Official Universal Orlando App!

After you have enjoyed one of the shows, proceed to the train station, snap a picture with the Conductor, and ride the Hogwarts Express back to King's Cross Station. (It is a completely different experience!)

Before going back inside Diagon Alley, explore the Streets of London. This is where you will find the Knight Bus (great interactive photo opportunity), 12 Grimmauld Place (Kreacher makes an appearance in the window from time-to-time), and the phone booth connecting you to the Ministry of Magic!

Now you can really explore Diagon Alley! Grab a Butterbeer to enjoy while you watch the Celestina Warbeck and the Banshees and The Tales of Beedle the Bard shows and explore the shops! The show times are available in The Official Universal Orlando App!

Don't miss Knockturn Alley! It has secret spell locations and the dark wizards' favorite shop, Borgin and Burkes.

Visit Shutterbutton's Photography Studio for your wizarding photo shoot that makes for a perfect keepsake of your magical day.

Have dinner at the Leaky Cauldron, but make sure you save room for dessert...

Florean Fortescue's Ice-Cream Parlour is a great place to find unique ice cream flavors. You won't find flavors like Butterbeer, Chocolate Chili, or Earl Grey & Lavender anywhere else!

At dusk, ride the Hogwarts Express back to Hogsmeade to watch the Nighttime Lights at Hogwarts Castle!

Wow! What a fun day of thrills, delicious food, Butterbeer, and spell casting... And you *still* have not experienced everything The Wizarding World of Harry Potter has to offer, so be sure to visit again!

WIZARDING WORLD CHALLENGE

	Completed
Have a Butterbeer!	
Ride all four Wizarding World rides! (Harry Potter and the Forbidden Journey, Flight of the Hippogriff, Hagrid's Magical Creatures Motorbike Adventure, Harry Potter and the Escape from Gringotts)	
Cast at least one spell in both Hogsmeade and Diagon Alley!	
Contact the Ministry of Magic!	
Find Kreacher!	
Take a picture with the Knight Bus Conductor!	
Practice your Parseltongue at the Magical Menagerie!	
Try on your house robe at Madam Malkins!	
Ride the Hogwarts Express both ways! *Don't forget to run through platform 9 ¾!*	
Take a picture in front of Hogwarts Castle!	
Visit the founders of Hogwarts inside the castle!	
Find the Marauders Map in Filch's Emporium!	
Watch one of the amazing Wizarding World shows!	
Take a picture in Hagrid's motorbike next to Gringotts!	
Find Professor Umbridge at Weasley Wizard Wheezes!	
Take a picture in front of Gringotts! *Bonus if you get the dragon spitting fire!*	
Find the Mimbulus Mimbletonia in Hogsmeade!	
Get some sweets at Honeydukes or Sugarplums!	
Find the door to the Daily Prophet in Diagon Alley!	
Find the wand that matches your birthday at Ollivanders!	
Have an ice cream at Florean Fortescue's!	
Take a picture in front of 12 Grimmauld Place!	

Complete the challenge during your vacation and post some pictures with the hashtag **#MMTWizardingChallenge**! Be sure to tag us on social media- **@MarvelousMouseTravels**!

FAQ'S

Do I need to read all the books and/or watch all the movies before visiting?

No! While it will definitely help you appreciate these incredibly themed lands more, you do not have to have read the books or watch the movies to enjoy the Wizarding World!

Do I need a park-to-park ticket?

Absolutely! A park-to-park ticket is the only way you will be able to experience the Hogwarts Express. It is a different experience each way!

What park should I start in?

If only visiting for one day, you should definitely start in the park that has Early Park Admission. Otherwise, we recommend starting in Universal Studios Florida in Diagon Alley, just like Harry did!

Can I wear house robes/cosplay?

Yes! You will see many others either dressed in robes or cosplaying characters. As long as you follow the Universal Studios' dress code, go for it!

Will I be able to meet Harry, Ron, Hermione, Dumbledore, etc?

While many characters are featured on the attractions, there is not any actual character meet and greets.

Do I need reservations to dine at the Three Broomsticks or The Leaky Cauldron?

Yes and no. You do not need reservations for lunch or dinner. Breakfast does require reservations; breakfast vouchers/reservations are included in the Harry Potter Exclusive Vacation Package or can be added to a regular vacation package.

Is an interactive wand better than a regular one?

The price difference is about $10, and we think it is worth the small difference to purchase an interactive wand. It will add to your entire experience, as you hunt for spell locations (including the hidden ones) and are able to cast spells and make magic happen around the Wizarding World.

If I get chosen during Ollivander's wand ceremony, do I have to purchase that wand?

No. You can purchase the wand that chooses you, choose your own, or not purchase anything... The choice is yours!

If my wand stops working, will Universal fix it?

Yes! Just bring your interactive wand to any of the wand shops, and they will work their magic to repair it for you, even if it was purchased on a previous trip.

Do Express Passes work in the Wizarding World?

At time of publication, Express Passes can be used on all rides in the Wizarding World except for Hagrid's Magical Creatures Motorbike Adventure. Therefore, they can be used on Harry Potter and the Forbidden Journey, Flight of the Hippogriff,

Hogwarts Express, and Harry Potter and the Escape from Gringotts.

How many days should I plan if I only want to visit the Wizarding World?

We suggest a minimum of two full days. There is so much to see and experience in the Wizarding World, you will need at least two days to explore!

Are there any special events in the Wizarding World?

Yes! During the Halloween season, you will be able to experience the Dark Arts at Hogwarts. There is a special nighttime projection show on Hogwarts Castle. There are also roaming death eaters that may just challenge you to a duel (only in Hogsmeade, beginning at dusk).

During the Holidays, Hogsmeade and Diagon Alley are all decked out in holiday decor! There is a special holiday themed projection show on Hogwarts Castle at night, The Magic of Christmas. You can also catch Celestina Warbeck singing a few holiday tunes in Carkitt Market.

What ages is the Wizarding World best for?

All ages! You do not have to know anything about Harry Potter to enjoy this incredibly themed and immersive world. Little ones can enjoy the shows, the shops, and all of the exciting sights and sounds. Older children, teens, and adults can take advantage of the thrill rides and food and drink options. If you want an extra special visit, a trip to the Wizarding World would be a perfect gift for an 11th birthday.

Is there anything special I can book in advance?

Yes! There is an Exclusive Harry Potter Vacation Package that includes breakfast vouchers for the Three Broomsticks, breakfast vouchers for The Leaky Cauldron, a photo session at Shutterbutton's, and a keepsake box with luggage tags. Ask your Marvelous Mouse Travels' agent about booking this vacation package!

BEST WIZARDING WORLD PHOTO SPOTS

- Hogwarts Castle-On the bridge between Hogsmeade and Jurassic Park
- In front of the Hogwarts Express in Hogsmeade
- Going through Platform 9 ¾ (traveling from King's Cross to Hogsmeade
- Perfume ad in King's Cross
- Hogwarts Castle- On the back patio of Three Broomsticks
- Butter Beer Barrel- Hogsmeade
- Gringotts dragon- Diagon Alley
- Love Potion Wall- Weasleys' Wizard Wheezes
- Knockturn Alley sign
- Vanishing Cabinet inside Borgin and Burkes
- Pink staircase inside Honeydukes
- Under the Wayfaring Wizards Welcomed sign
- Skelegrow window- Diagon Alley
- Knight Bus- both the back and in the front with the conductor
- 12 Grimmauld Place door
- Dr. Filibuster's fireworks wall
- With Pygmy Puffs inside Weasleys' Wizard Wheezes
- Inside the red phone booth
- On Hagrid's Motorbike by Gringotts Bank
- Under the "Please Respect the Spell Limits" Hogsmeade Sign
- In the Gringotts' lobby

CONCLUSION

We hope you not only learned a lot about the Wizarding World of Harry Potter, but we hope you are now even more excited for your trip to Universal Orlando Resort. Hopefully you are now fully prepared to cast spells, escape from Gringotts, choose your wand, walk through Platform 9 ¾, and finally visit the one place that will always be there to welcome you home, Hogwarts.

A LOOK AHEAD

Universal Orlando Resort is expanding with a fourth park. This new park, Epic Universe, will be located 10-15 minutes away from the current Universal campus. This will be the first of Universal's parks to feature a hub and spoke design, which will allow each land to be totally immersive (just like Diagon Alley)! Only one of the new lands has been confirmed so far, Super Nintendo World, but there are rumors of a Harry Potter-themed land, as well.

The Wizarding World of Harry Potter (Rumored)
This land is rumored to have two attractions. The first will represent the British Ministry of Magic, complete with Floo Network fireplaces. The second will represent the French Ministry of Magic as seen in *Fantastic Beasts and Where to Find Them*. As of January 2021, new rumors indicate that one of the rides would give Harry Potter fans a chance to fly on a broomstick! Universal also recently released a patent for a virtual reality experience in the French Ministry of Magic part. The experience will come with a VR headset, motion base, and interactive controls.

THE MARVELOUS DIFFERENCE

Here at Marvelous Mouse Travels, we LOVE Universal. We share in our clients' excitement, as we plan each unique vacation and help create unforgettable memories. When you use a Marvelous Mouse Travels' agent, you can trust that your vacation is in the best hands.

We are the recipient of Universal's Top Travel Agency award for 2019 and, in 2021, was recognized as a Preferred Diamond Agency. We are the first agency, and currently the only agency, to hold this distinction from Universal in the nation. We also frequently travel to Universal Orlando Resort for on-site trainings hosted by Universal; our most recent agency training was in November 2021, and we have had agents training individually on-site throughout the year. All of our agents also frequently visit the parks, so they can stay up-to-date with new information, practices, and tips. We do the work… You have the fun!

We cannot wait to help you plan your next Universal Orlando Resort adventure! As a reminder, our travel planning services are completely free to you! So, what are you waiting for? Let's get you connected with a Universal expert today!

If you would like to be connected to a Marvelous Mouse Travels' agent, you can visit our website- www.MarvelousMouseTravels.com/ContactUs

Be sure to also follow us on social media!

Instagram: @MarvelousMouseTravels
Facebook: Marvelous Mouse Travels
TikTok: @MarvelousMouseTravels

MORE FUN

Wizarding World Favorites

When We Visited:	Where We Stayed:

Who We Went With:

Favorite Snacks	Favorite Spells Cast

Favorite Ride	Favorite Show

Favorite Type of Butterbeer	Hogwarts House

Favorite Souvenir	Favorite Shop

Favorite Memory

My Wizarding World Bucket List

- [ ]
- [ ]
- [ ]
- [ ]
- [ ]
- [ ]
- [ ]
- [ ]
- [ ]
- [ ]
- [ ]
- [ ]
- [ ]
- [ ]
- [ ]
- [ ]
- [ ]

ADDITIONAL RESOURCES

For planning tips and tricks beyond the Wizarding World, you can purchase our 600+ page e-book, "*A Marvelous Guide to Universal Orlando*" on our website-
www.MarvelousMouseTravels.com

Some of the exciting and useful information you will find in this e-book:
How to Access Early Park Admission
First Timer Mistakes to Avoid
Money Saving Tips
Height/Weight Requirements for Attractions
Best Times to Visit
Insider Tips and Tricks
Restaurant/Food/Drink Recommendations
Hotel Comparisons
Ticket Options
Fun and Interesting Facts
Ride Intensity Meters
Park Touring Itineraries
Best Photo Locations throughout the Parks
Drinking Across the Universe
Universal with Kids
A *MUST HAVE* Comprehensive Guide to The Wizarding World of Harry Pooter Including:
Itinerary, Wand Guide, Easter Eggs, and tips for fans of the books and movies!
Universal for Adults
Special Events throughout the Year
COVID Guidelines and Policies

Printed in Great Britain
by Amazon